Earthmovers

By Kenny Allen

Gareth Stevens
Publishing

Please visit our website, www.garethstevens.com. For a free color catalog of all our high-quality books, call toll free 1-800-542-2595 or fax 1-877-542-2596.

Library of Congress Cataloging-in-Publication Data

Allen, Kenny, 1971-
Earthmovers / Kenny Allen.
    p. cm. — (Monster machines)
Includes index.
ISBN 978-1-4339-7168-6 (pbk.)
ISBN 978-1-4339-7169-3 (6-pack)
ISBN 978-1-4339-7167-9 (library binding)
1. Earthmoving machinery—Juvenile literature. I. Title.
TA725.A45 2012
621.8'65—dc23

                        2011043760

First Edition

Published in 2013 by
Gareth Stevens Publishing
111 East 14th Street, Suite 349
New York, NY 10003

Copyright © 2013 Gareth Stevens Publishing

Designer: Daniel Hosek
Editor: Greg Roza

Photo credits: Cover, p. 1 isifa/Getty Images; borders Norebbo/Shutterstock.com; p. 5 Frank Jr/ Shutterstock.com; p. 7 © iStockphoto.com/ewg3D; p. 9 Dmitry Kalinovsky/Shutterstock.com; p. 11 kaband/Shutterstock.com; p. 13 Zacarias Pereira de Mata/Shutterstock.com; p. 15 iStockphoto/Thinkstock.com; p. 17 Levent Konuk/Shutterstock.com; p. 19 Hemera/ Thinkstock.com; p. 21 saasemen/Shutterstock.com.

Printed in the United States of America

CPSIA compliance information: Batch #CS12GS: For further information contact Gareth Stevens, New York, New York at 1-800-542-2595.

Contents

Boldface words appear in the glossary.

Meet the Movers

Have you ever watched the machines at a **construction** site? They growl and roar. They dig giant holes. They carry loads too heavy for smaller **vehicles**. They're earthmovers! These monster machines need to be big to get big jobs done.

5

Right Tool for the Job

Construction workers use earthmovers to prepare land for new buildings. **Mining** companies use them to dig deep holes and carry dirt and rock away. They're also used to make roads.

7

Bulldozers

Bulldozers are large tractors. A bulldozer has two tracks that allow it to move on soft dirt. It has a large plate in front called a blade. The blade pushes dirt and rock and makes the ground flat.

9

Wheel Loaders

Wheel loaders have large buckets. They **scoop** up dirt, rocks, sand, and even snow. The load is dumped into another machine so it can be moved. A wheel loader has four big wheels for getting around.

11

Dump Trucks

Dump trucks carry heavy loads. They **haul** rock, dirt, sand, and pieces of broken buildings. Sometimes they carry snow or logs, too. The box on the back of a dump truck tips up to dump out its load.

13

Scrapers

Scrapers make the ground flat and smooth. The back part is called the hopper. A blade under the hopper scrapes the ground as the machine moves. The blade scoops up dirt and rock and puts them in the hopper.

15

Graders

Graders are needed to make roads. They're used after bulldozers and scrapers take away most of the dirt. A grader has a long blade. The blade makes the ground perfectly flat as it moves forward.

17

Excavators

Excavators have a long, moveable arm with a bucket at the end. They're used to dig holes, move heavy things, and knock down old buildings. Excavators can have tracks or wheels.

The Bagger 293

The Bagger 293 is a bucket-wheel excavator used to mine coal. It's the largest earthmover in the world! It has a giant wheel with buckets on it. When the wheel turns, the buckets dig up more dirt and rock than any other earthmover can!

Getting to Know the Bagger

- The Bagger 293 is the largest and heaviest land vehicle in the world.

- It's about as tall as a 30-story building.

- It takes 5 people to run the Bagger 293.

- The wheel is 71 feet (21.6 m) wide.

- The wheel has 18 buckets. Each bucket can hold as much dirt as 80 bathtubs!

Glossary

construction: having to do with the act of building something

haul: to pull or carry something heavy

mining: having to do with digging something out of the ground

scoop: to reach under something and lift it

vehicle: something that carries people or goods, such as a car or plane

For More Information

Books

Doman, Mary Kate. *Earthmovers and Diggers*. Berkeley Heights, NJ: Enslow Publishers, 2012.

Hill, Lee Sullivan. *Earthmovers*. Minneapolis, MN: Lerner Publications, 2011.

Williams, Linda D. *Earthmovers*. Mankato, MN: Capstone Press, 2005.

Websites

Extreme Machines
www.worsleyschool.net/science/files/extreme/machines.html
Learn more about the machines in this book, as well as other monster machines, and see pictures.

How Caterpillar Backhoe Loaders Work
science.howstuffworks.com/transport/engines-equipment/ backhoe-loader.htm
Read about the backhoe—a monster machine that is a combination of a bulldozer, loader, and excavator.

Index